Explore
Durham by Car

Explore
Durham by Car

by
Jack Hanmer

Dalesman Books
1987

The Dalesman Publishing Company Ltd.,
Clapham, via Lancaster, LA2 8EB

First published 1987

ISBN: 0 85206 898 0

Printed by Smiths of Bradford, England

CONTENTS

Cover photograph of the Old Bridge, Durham City, by Tom Parker.

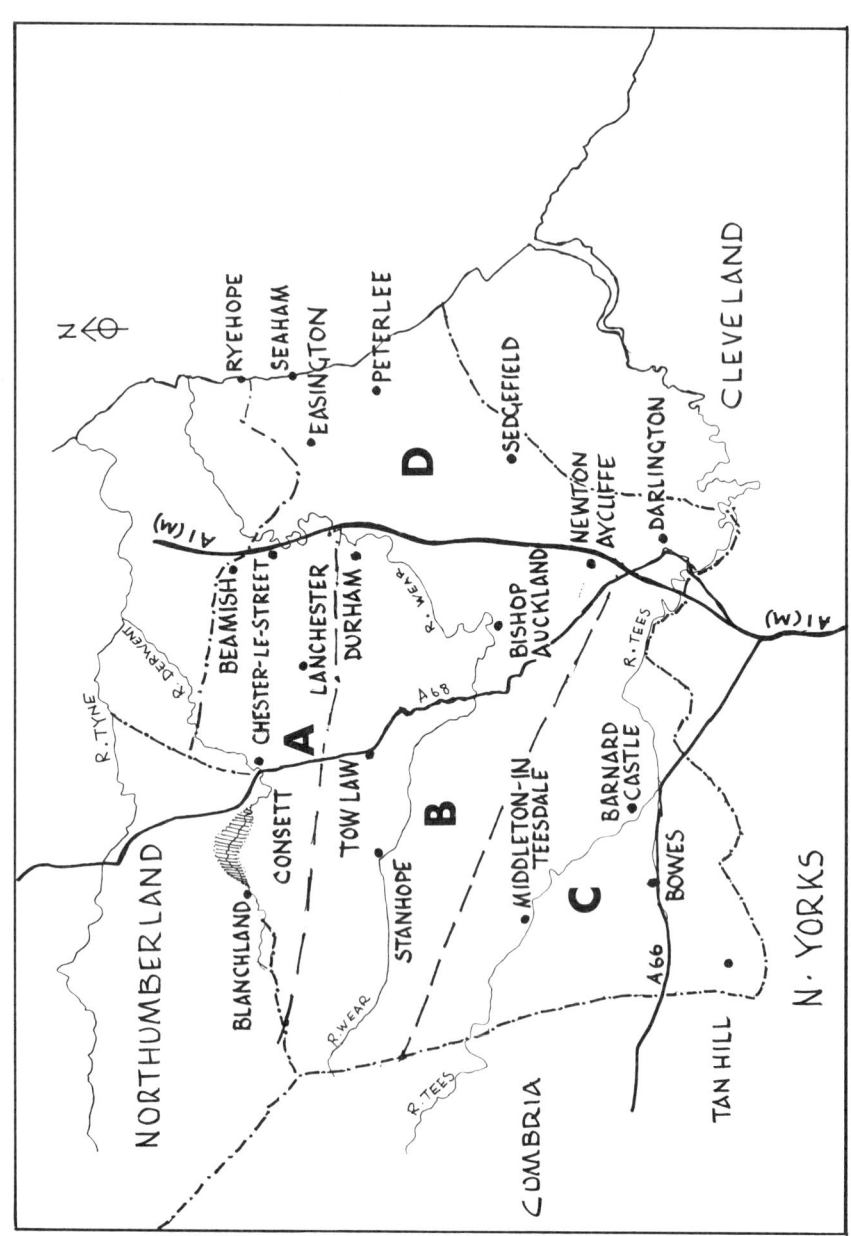

Introduction

Transition might well be the key word to any consideration of County Durham during the latter half of the twentieth century. The two faces which the county has for many years presented to the visitor have at the same time been its downfall and its charm. On the industrial front the heavy basic industries have scarred the landscape with unsightly tips of varying constituents which have not exactly endeared themselves to the tourist. There are those who asserted that the best view of Consett at night was from the A68 with furnaces ablaze with ethereal glow. Away from all this and by way of compensation are the rolling acres of scenic grandeur which compare favourably with neighbouring Cumbria, Northumberland and Yorkshire. And set firmly between these contrasting aspects is the jewel of the county - Durham City - which for centuries has been the Mecca of the pilgrim and, more recently, of the tourist.

By the turn of this century much of the industrial legacy described above will have given way to vistas more pleasing to the eye. An enthusiastic and equally energetic County Council has been winning awards from numerous bodies for the excellent reclamation and conservation work which it has so far undertaken. Fortunately, the work continues and it may be that one day the only sign of the Durham of yesteryear will be in places like the Beamish Open Air Museum. This latter has received world wide acclaim for its contribution to industrial and sociological heritage. In contrast to Beamish are the modern towns of Peterlee and Newton Aycliffe, and on a philosophical note one can contemplate whether the acquisition of 'all mod cons' has made life any happier for those who now have them.

Before reorganisation played havoc with boundaries it would have been apt to describe the coastline as lying 'twixt Tyne and Tees'. Today a much reduced coastline lies between the Pincushion Rocks below Ryhope and Crimdon Beck above Hartlepool. In the south the Tees forms the boundary around Yarm and the Middletons, whilst to the west the county borders on Cumbria where in fact the Tees rises in the Pennines.

Four well-known trunk roads traverse the county, the more familiar being the A1(M) which has replaced, in less colourful style, the Great North Road. The A68 is the back way into Scotland via Carter Bar and the notorious A66 - one of the first to be blocked when snow is about - travels west from Scotch Corner into Cumbria. The A19, much improved, carries heavy traffic to and from the industrial centres of Tyne and Wear and Cleveland.

It has seemed convenient to divide the county into four main areas leaving Durham City to enjoy a chapter to itself. The first takes in the northern part of the county and includes Chester-le-Street, Consett, Stanley and Beamish. The second covers Weardale and also Crook, Bishop Auckland and Shildon. The third area runs up Teesdale from Barnard Castle and down to the Yorkshire border whilst the fourth, which includes Darlington, covers all the county which lies east of the A1(M). Finally, a short appendix lists the Country Parks, Nature Walks and the like, all designed to take the visitors into rural Durham.

Whilst it is never possible to include all the hamlets and villages in a book of this size, it is hoped that those which are will reflect the various aspects of County Durham. One wonders, when the transformation is complete, which particular facets of 'the good old days' will actually be missed. Only time will tell.

The writer is grateful for all the generous assistance which many people gave during the research period. In particular, the staff at County Hall and in the various outposts of that empire were extremely helpful.

BEAMISH

8

Durham City

The records inform us that Durham has the third oldest university in England and 'the grandest Norman Cathedral in Christendom', but statistics cannot convey the true splendour of this ancient city. Its very position high above a loop of the Wear has caused the cathedral to become a landmark which warrants the familiar cliche 'once seen never forgotten' and from it one can tour the city. Even supposing ecclesiastical history is not your particular forte you will be hard pressed not to admire, in all its various aspects, the final resting place of St. Cuthbert from whom the cathedral takes its name.

The magnificent edifice is often first seen from the window of a train as it rumbles over the viaduct or maybe from one of the approaches by road to the city centre. It is not until one is actually on Palace Green that the full majesty of the building is really appreciated. But there is more to come. Once inside the Cathedral the true splendour of the place becomes apparent and it should be said that to see it all will take a considerable amount of your time. In fact, you could spend a whole day around Palace Green leaving the remainder of the city to be explored on another occasion. Since the only Cathedral restaurant to appear in the Good Food Guide is at Durham there is no excuse for having to interrupt what will probably be many hours of exciting exploration in these parts. As with so many places of interest a little preliminary reading will pay dividends. Nothing frustrates more than to return home to discover what you didn't discover whilst you were actually there.

The list of attractions is quite long: the nave, the Neville Screen, the font cover, the raised throne, the Galilee Chapel, the Frosterley Marble, the museum, the tombs of St. Cuthbert and the Venerable Bede - and still much more. There are two quite interesting and obviously related aspects to the city. On the ecclesiastical side is the history of the See itself from the time in 762 when records show that a Bishop was consecrated. Later in 995 monks carrying the body of St. Cuthbert came across Dunholm and chose the spot for his final resting place. Three years later they began work on their Saxon cathedral but it was Bishop Ralph Flambard who in 1093 began work on the present cathedral. It was 'completed' in 1133 except for the Galilee Chapel, the Chapel of Nine Altars and the central tower which were later additions. Flambard was responsible for much of the Durham we know today including the clearing of dwellings from Palace Green and the building of Framwellgate Bridge. Built as a gateway to his new suburb of Framwell Gate it was largely rebuilt some 300 years later by Cardinal Langley.

From time to time Bishops of Durham have been in the news and perhaps none more frequently than the present incumbent whose utterances of late have caused palpitations in certain quarters. Home of the Bishops was the Castle, also on Palace Green. After the Conquest it was bestowed by William on the first Prince Bishop - Walcher, and not until 1832, when Bishop van Mildert bestowed it on the university, did it cease to be the Bishop's residence. (This is now at Bishop Auckland). Though now very much a part of the university it is still open to the public and certainly worth visiting. Amongst the various items of architectural interest are: the Gatehouse, the Great Hall, the black staircase, the fifteenth century kitchens, the Tunstall Chapel and, the most inner of inner sanctums, the windowless Norman crypt chapel. There are guided tours at frequent intervals during the day.

The university appears to have occupied the remaining buildings of Palace Green which began life as courts, hospitals, town houses and almshouses. In spite of its inevitable role as a car park, Palace Green does retain that air of tranquillity so often missing from our inner cities. It sets the scene as it were for further exploration of the city, a task which takes one along footpaths and vennels (alleys), some of which descend to the river. Surrounded as it is on three sides by the Wear, the riverside walks are very popular and picturesque. From the west bank by the weir and the cornmill, the view on the far bank is of South Street with its Georgian town houses. The river itself is now crossed by four pedestrianised bridges or footbridges - Framwell Gate, Elvet, Kingsgate and Prebends - and from them the June regatta can be viewed to advantage. Boats may be hired from Elvet riverside where stands the former House of Correction. Its modern counterpart, H. M. Prison, lies behind the Assize courts of New Elvet.

Both North Bailey and Saddler Street contain interesting houses and lead down to the market place in the centre of which stands 'the horse', the affectionate term for the equestrian statue of the Marquis of Londonderry. He it was who, after receiving distinction in both military and political spheres, applied himself to domestic issues and founded Seaham Harbour. The Church of St. Nicholas, rebuilt in 1858, stands on the site of a former Norman church and contains a stone font which once saw service as a bird bath in someone's garden! The Guildhall dates from 1356 and is the oldest of the civic buildings whereas the Town Hall is much younger, 1851, and shares with the old Duston Station the architect, Philip Hardwick. Running south-west down to Framwellgate Bridge, Silver Street has retained much of its original character with the Tudor fronted shops. In sharp contrast the Milburngate shopping centre, across the bridge, presents what some have described as the impersonal aspect of twentieth century architecture.

Durham City, unlike York, does not have the multiplicity of churches which adorn that place, but after the cathedral and St. Nicholas, you will find others which are worth a visit. They are: the twelfth century St. Margaret of Antioch in Crossgate; St Mary the Less in South Bailey, also twelfth century as too is St Oswald's in Church Street; and St Mary le Bow on the North Bailey, which dates from the seventeenth century.

DURHAM . . .

The Tourist Information Centre which might well be your first port of call if you are to embark on any pre-exploratory reading can be seen from the market place. It is located at the beginning of Claypath, Number 13, across the busy inner ring road, and the usual array of information pamphlets and booklets such as 'City Centre Walk' are available. The National Trust gift and information shop, also popular with tourists, is located in Saddler Street, an area which tends to become busy with people plying to and from Palace Green. Market days in the city are Thursday, Friday and Saturday, whilst Wednesday is the early closing day for those shops which still follow custom.

Moving now beyond the immediate area of Palace Green and the market place, John Betjeman would have had something interesting to say about ring roads and 'concrete monstrosities' which are in conflict with what we have so far been admiring. Nevertheless, we can find a number of historical buildings in various parts of the city which are worth discovering. The tythe barn at the corner of Hallgarth Street and Whinney Hill is medieval and belonged originally to the Priory. The Kepier Hospital has a medieval arch and buildings but it is not open for viewing. Old Elvet, running south-east from Elvet Bridge, is still graced by dignified Georgian facades and was originally the main route south and until quite recently this broad thoroughfare was the venue for horse fairs. Today it is known by millions of television viewers as the place where leading politicians of a certain persuasion adorn a balcony before joining the procession to the former Smiddyhaughs (Smith's riverside fields) and Durham Racecourse. This is the famous Durham Miners' Gala held on the third Saturday in July and very popular it is.

Vying with the cathedral is the university which too has an interesting history. Durham Hall, Oxford, was an endowed college as long ago as 1380 but it was 1833 before nineteen scholars under Archdeacon Thorp founded the university in Durham City. With some justification the College Hall in Bishops Castle is thought to be more beautiful than any at Oxford. Bede College for men and St Hilda's for women were established as Anglican training colleges. Expansion away from the peninsula was inevitable and perhaps the best known of these 'out of town' buildings is the Gulbenkian Museum of Oriental Art. Open to the public it contains rare treasures being the only museum in Britain devoted to Oriental art. Collingwood College across the way has the distinction of being the first to be founded as a mixed College and many of the college buildings have blended successfully with the wooded grounds of the site of Oswald House.

The key to a map of Durham lists 36 buildings or places of historical interest and still there are others. In more recent times a number of modern buildings have been erected and functional rather than aesthetic would be the term many would use. To the north at Aykley Heads is the Durham Light Infantry Museum and Arts Centre where two hundred years of history of the Regiment is displayed.

Beyond this at the top of the hill is County Hall where the warmth and personality of those who are beavering away within its austere walls is in sharp contrast with the impersonal nature of the building. Murals, a mosaic and some sculptures which are to be found at County Hall tell the story of Durham - city and county.

Durham is a city of contrasts which will not be fully appreciated in haste and to which you will most certainly want to return.

A. North Durham

This most northern region of County Durham contains a variety of scenery: the peace and quiet of Derwent and the hustle and bustle of the towns which are left – some having been lost to Tyne and Wear when re-organisation took place. Beamish is perhaps the most visited attraction in these parts. It is a place where time has stood still but not so for much of the area where change is all round. The demise of long standing traditional industries and the introduction of new ones is very much in evidence. The Derwent marks the boundary at Blanchland, where the best view of this attractive Northumberland village is from the Durham side of the river.

Derwent Reservoir
On the border between the A68 and the B6306.
The B6306 takes you from Blanchland to Edmondbyers on the southern shore of the reservoir. A minor road left at Carricks picnic area follows the northern shore and it is on this road that information boards about wild fowl have been erected in the area of the nature reserve. The sailing club and the Millshield picnic area are also located on the northern shore.

Pow Hill Country Park, the largest recreational area, 45 acres, is on the B6303 and from the elevated car park the views across the water are extensive. There is also a bird hide for watchers and some 24,000 trees if children want to play hide and seek. The Country Park is managed by the County Council and is very popular, especially at weekends. The utilities building from which fishing permits are available is located on the approach to the dam which has a one way traffic flow. Altogether a place where people in nearby towns can really get away from it all if only to relax and breathe invigorating country air.

Edmundbyers (alternatively Edmondbyers)
At the junction of the B6306 and B6278 south of Derwent Reservoir.
This moorland village has been described as being surrounded by heather and sheep which is really no bad thing. The Burnhope Burn below the village is a tributary of the Derwent. If you pursue the history of the small church – founded in the twelfth century but restored in 1859 – you will discover what appears to be a hotch potch of contributions in wood. Auckland and Durham castles and the cathedral all supplied wood of various origins in the seventeenth century to help restore the interior. The village is thought to have been a meeting place of local witches in the seventeenth and eighteenth centuries. From Edmondbyers the minor road running south off the B6278 passes through Muggleswick and on to the A68.

Castleside

At the junction of the A68 and A692 immediately west of Consett.

This village could be best described as a 'frontier place' for it is on the edge of all that is pleasant in the county with its back, as it were, to the industrial scene. The Smelters Arms, located at the junction of the road out from Consett, with the A68, reflects this former industrial wealth. The juxtaposition of town and country which is so apparent here is repeated many times as you journey through County Durham.

Consett

On the A692 from Gateshead just west of Ledgate, the junction of the A691 from Durham.

September 1980 is not a month to be remembered with affection in Consett. Over 100 years of iron and steel production came to an end at that time and travellers on the A68, the 'Carter Bar Road', would no longer witness the hissing, steaming and glowing of the great Vulcan forges. Today they are gone and the vast acres of emptiness are being transformed into industrial estates, a leisure complex and aesthetically pleasing landscapes. There are, in fact, a number of small industrial estates in the immediate surrounds of Consett. The town is not one of Durham's gems which may explain why an eye-catching red-bricked bus station is perhaps trying to redress the balance. It has to be said that it has its critics. The centre of the town has a well patronised shopping area, an indoor swimming pool with sauna baths and a sizeable sports centre. The parish church is of Norman design though not that ancient, merely 1862, whilst the Roman Catholic church of Saint Patrick, 1959, has a brick built basilican form and is probably Consett's most interesting building. The offices of the Derwentside District are in the familiar modern concrete guise on Medomsley Road.

History of any consequence is more likely to be found in the suburbs of the town, for example, at Shotley Bridge; there were swords being fashioned by a colony of German migrants in the seventeenth century. One of their cottages dated 1691 has an inscription over its door which, translated, runs: 'The blessing of the Lord makes you rich without care so long as you are industrious in your calling and do what is required of you'. The Quakers were in evidence both at Shotley Bridge and nearby Benfieldside where in 1653 one of England's first Meeting Houses was established. Saint Cuthbert's parish church was designed by John Dobson, planner of much of Newcastle. At Blackhill is a Cheshire Home in what was formerly a nineteenth century hospital. Leadgate has the stamp of a worker's village which was in fact its original purpose. The uncommon Saint Ives gave his name to the church which would have been attended by both coal miners and iron workers. The nineteenth century Roman Catholic centre established at Leadgate was well known nationally. At Crook Hall, just south of Leadgate, are the remains of a seminary which was established by French refugees from the Napoleonic Wars. They later moved

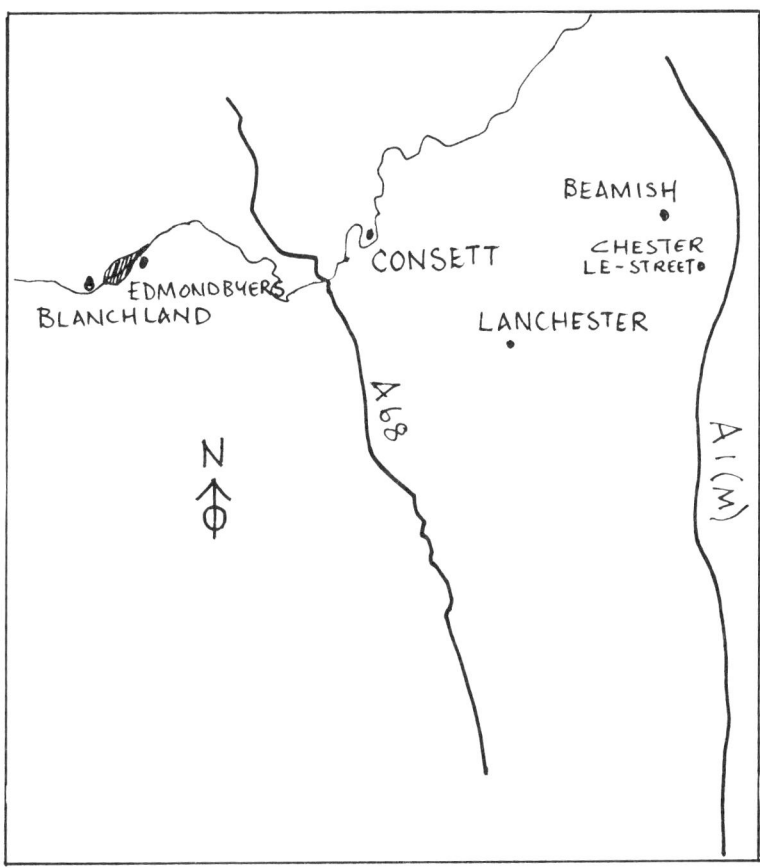

to a new home at Ushaw College. Still on matters ecclesiastical and not quite so widely known is the fact that Consett's Salvation Army Band was that church's first when formed in 1879.

Lanchester

On the A691 between Durham and Consett.
A short by-pass has taken the bulk of heavy traffic round the back of Lanchester so that some semblance of normality pervades the main street. The village took its name from the Roman long fort, Longovicium, established to the west, but since it was never thoroughly excavated it has not achieved the popularity of other Roman encampments. Other evidence of things historical include: the site of a reservoir fed by two four-mile-long aqueducts, the remains of a Roman road which ran to Hadrian's Wall and to York and what must be the ultimate in

'fishy' stories. A local farmer fishing in Smallhope Burn 'hooked' a sword, four scythes and eight axe heads, all of Anglo-Saxon origin! Some artefacts are to be found in the imposing All Saints Church – the altar with an AD244 date inscribed is in the south porch and the pillars of the north arcade are also Roman. The chancel of the church is largely thirteenth century, the tower fifteenth century and some 700 year old ironwork adorns the door of the south porch.

Two of Lanchester's sons who achieved a degree of fame were John Hodgson and William Greenwell. The former came to the village as a young man to run the local school, then became ordained and eventually began to write poetry when not engaged upon history and archaeology!

Greenwell, a more distinguished archaeologist, was a true son, having been born at Greenwell Ford, the old house above the River Browney. He eventually became a canon and librarian of Durham Cathedral and by way of a hobby took up fishing. He was 97 when he died in 1919.

The 4,000 inhabitants of Lanchester might well comtemplate the 'fate' of Corbridge which, because the Roman connection was exploited, is invaded constantly by devotees of that culture.

Stanley
At the junction of the A693 from the A1(M) and the A6076 running south from Gateshead.

Lying midway between Consett and Chester-le-Street, Stanley now gives the impression of being a fairly modern town. At first glance its pedestrianised town centre precinct has the hall mark of a Peterlee or Newton Aycliffe whereas in fact it goes back a long way. When the Romans were in evidence in these parts in the second and third centuries, they established a cattle compound in order to feed their forts at Newcastle and South Shields. They also constructed a causeway between the town and the forts passing through, appropriately, Causey and crossing Watling Street.

It was the discovery of an abundance of good quality coking coal early in the eighteenth century that transformed the village into a sizeable colliery town. Tragically two mining disasters left their mark on Stanley. In 1909 some 168 men and boys lost their lives and just after World War II in 1947 an underground explosion at the Louisa pit killed 22 miners. The name is remembered in the Louisa Sports Centre and a granite monument at the entrance to East Stanley cemetery recalls the earlier disaster.

The town has not been devoid of churches, there being originally a fair number of Nonconformist chapels, a nineteenth century parish church and a Roman Catholic church which was restored and enlarged in 1909. Today, a new temple accommodates 'worshippers' of a different complexion. This is the vast supermarket which is patronised by people from a wide area as too is the bowls centre on the upper storey. Because leisure is so much a part of life today it is no surprise to discover that Stanley, like other towns with declining industries, has excellent facilities. In the sixties new buildings included the Public Library, the multi-purpose Civic Hall and a covered swimming pool. Indoor bowls, a sports centre, three golf courses within reasonable distance of the town and a greyhound track complete the picture.

Approaching Stanley from Beamish, the description 'hill top town' appears apt.

Beamish Open Air Museum

On a minor road which runs between the A693 and the A6076 north-east of Stanley.

The publicity informs you that you don't visit Beamish, you experience it. Since it is probably the finest museum of social and industrial life at the turn of the century it is no surprise that its attendance record is only surpassed by Durham cathedral.

It is not a static museum for things really do happen at Beamish so that it is at the same time both entertaining and educational. No television programme or book, however well presented and written, could convey the atmosphere which is created by people actually engaged on tasks of yesteryear. Bread baked in a coal fired oven, old trams and steam engines, the 'Co-op', the pub and the station all contribute to help you make that nostalgic journey back in time. Taking a number 342 tram to the corner shop, watching the miner clean up in the tin bath on the hearth, or visiting the pit cottages, all evoke comments like: 'just how it wer' when I wer' a lad'.

Four hours is the minimum time needed to see all that Beamish has to offer, but all day would soon pass, particularly if children become absorbed in the

BEAMISH.

activities – rides on the Victorian fairground and seeing the animals down on the farm.

The man whose dream it was, Frank Atkinson, has devoted the last 33 years to creating a time-warp street which has aptly been described as 'a nostalgic shrine for the elderly and a history lesson for the young'.

The adjacent Beamish Hall houses a popular introductory exhibition including the famous Durham quilts and pottery demonstrations during the summer season. Beamish is very much alive and a 'must' on anyone's itinerary which covers the North-East.

Causey Arch
Off the A6076 north of Stanley.

Literally 'just up the road' from Beamish (take the minor roads from the museum towards Tanfield). This is reported to be the world's oldest surviving railway bridge. It is located in Causey Wood in what is now a picnic site and was originally a wooden structure which, as one might have expected, collapsed. The architect, coincidentally Ralph Wood, replaced it with a stone arch about which he was not very optimistic and is said to have killed himself, so worried was he that it too would collapse. Some 250 years later it still stands – a memorial to his skill!

Tanfield Railway
Five miles south-west of Gateshead on the A6076.

A visit to Causey Woods could be combined with a look at what progress is being made at the Tanfield Railway site. This is an example, much repeated nationwide, of how enthusiastic volunteers give of their time and skill to restore former railway lines.

The village of Tanfield away to the west of the Arch and the railway has historical connections with the Conqueror. Its parish church, restored in 1853, was founded around 900 AD by monks from Chester-le-Street. The hall, which dates from the seventeenth and eighteenth centuries, has a fine staircase and wrought-iron exterior gates which are quite beautiful. It is not open to the public.

Chester-le-Street
On the A167 six miles north of Durham.

It is not easy to appreciate when driving through the town that historically it can compete with Durham City. When the monks of Lindisfarne sallied forth in 875 AD with the body of Saint Cuthbert they were rather peripatetic until, in 882 AD, they came to Chester-le-Street and established a church on the site of a Roman camp. In ecclesiastical terms this was a cathedral and for 113 years the town found itself at the centre of religious activity over a vast diocese. It was the seat of nine Saxon Bishops but when the Saint's body was removed to Durham

– via Ripon incidentally – the church and the town declined in importance.

Bishop Egelric founded a new church just prior to the Norman Conquest and it was this church which, after numerous restorations, became the town's parish church. Its spire rises 189 feet from the octagon tower and is thought to be the finest in the county. It was whilst the foundations for the church were being dug that the Roman connection was confirmed. The hoard of gold which was discovered was used by the Bishop in distant Peterborough and, for his misdeed, he was imprisoned in the Tower. The Roman garrison gave its name to the town – a camp on the main route – which many will remember with affection as the Great North Road. The more modern dual carriageway A1(M) seems not to evoke the same feelings of affection as the great turnpikes of yesteryear and we must accept this as the price we have to pay for progress.

Chester-le-Street today has much in common with towns in similar situations: an interesting history, a more recent rise and fall of industrial activity, a focal point for a number of satellite villages and attempts to give it a new look to meet the changing pattern of life as we move towards the end of the twentieth century.

Across the river and to the east lie the areas of recreation and the two notable landmarks – Lumley Castle and Lambton Castle. The approach to Lumley is by the town's playing fields and golf club. The building dates from the fourteenth century, though the family history can be traced to Saxon times. At the turn of this century the castle was refurbished and then occupied by the tenth Earl of Scarborough. After a period as a hall of residence for Durham university it was transformed into a conference centre and hotel with a very popular attraction – Elizabethan banquets. The accommodation is described as 'unique' since this is no ordinary hotel and, as befits the image, four-poster beds are common place.

B. Weardale

Stretching from Bishop Auckland to the Cumbrian boundary, Weardale is one of Durham's more popular areas and is much visited. The Wear is one of the north-east's great rivers and much of the area's beauty lies along its route as it winds down from the bleak Northern Pennines, fed by numerous burns, to the Aucklands before heading north to Durham City.

As with other areas of outstanding beauty there is a conflict of interest between the conservationist and the industrialist and in more than one place the landscape suffers. 'Bishop' and Crook are the only towns of any size but the villages which lie on the river are pleasant and usually contain some interesting facet which is worth exploring.

To the south lies the sister dale of Tees which is described in the next section and which is reached by climbing one of several moorland roads. The views from these are far reaching and you will not be surprised to learn that in a severe winter many of the isolated hamlets and farmsteads are snow bound.

Before travelling into Weardale proper we will look at some of the towns and villages which lie to the east and where much of England's industrial and ecclesiastical heritage lies.

Newton Aycliffe

On the A167 five miles north of Darlington.

There is always an interesting comparison to be made between the New Towns in Britain. The older company towns of Bourneville and Port Sunlight make a striking contrast with Harlow, East Kilbride, Milton Keynes and here, in Durham, Peterlee and Newton Aycliffe. This latter had the distinction of being the first designated New Town in the North in 1947 and somewhat different in that it was not an overspill town. Its original purpose was to provide housing for the workers on the huge industrial estate which was being developed on the site of the former Royal Ordnance Factory. The target population has been increased from an initial 10,000 to 27,000 in 1980 and an eventual 'official' figure of 35,000, though some forecasts suggest 45,000.

Its name was derived from 'oak trees', there being an abundance of these in earlier times and the town is now incorporated into the District of Sedgefield. A series of 'villages' within the larger connurbation helped to dispel the notion that this is one huge soulless housing estate and there is a mix of both private and council properties. Whilst these show a variety of design – traditional and non-traditional, bungalows and terraced – there are no tower blocks to offend the eye.

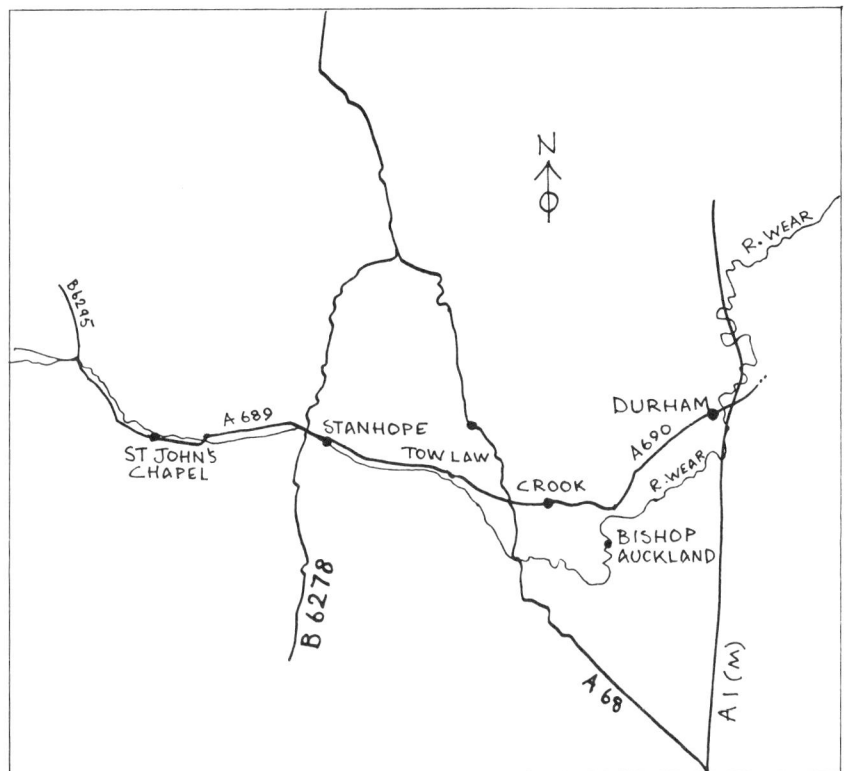

There is a central shopping centre which differs from Peterlee in both design and comfort – there are not so many gusty corners. In practice, the huge hyper-markets and 'famous names' stores of nearby Darlington exert quite a strong pull in the matter of shopping.

East of the A167, which many will remember as the Great North Road, stands Newton Aycliffe school which has for years been one of Britain's best known schools for the treatment of offenders. Quite separately and south-west of the town is School Aycliffe which is a hospital for the mentally ill.

The old village of Aycliffe lies across the A167 and its Saxon church, after the manner of Escomb, is one of Durham's oldest.

Heighington

On a minor road running due west from Aycliffe village.
The busy A6072 from Darlington to Bishop Auckland now by-passes the village and this helps considerably in restoring the peace and quiet which was formerly enjoyed.

It is an ideal place for a walkabout with much to interest the visitor who will be smitten with the spacious green which, being some 500 feet above sea level, affords excellent views. It is not difficult to imagine the villagers drying their bleached cloth on the greens in times past.

The focal point is St Michael's and All Angels Norman church to which additions were added in the thirteenth, sixteenth and nineteenth centuries. A marble monument of Captain Cumby, RN, reminds one of the Trafalgar link when the illustrious officer sank a French ship. His descendants still live in the appropriately named, Trafalgar House, one of several houses of character which adorn the environs; Redworth Hall a mile to the north, and Middridge Grange, another mile beyond that, being two others. In the village itself are a number of older houses which one might seek out: the eighteenth century house formerly a private grammar school, the old manor house 1620, and Eldon House, these latter being on East Green. Across the West Green is the Bay Horse, a seventeenth century inn, the other hostelry being the George and Dragon. The duck pond was filled in, no doubt to save more children and inebriated fathers from falling in. The stone pant was erected by a local vicar in the early 1800s and it still stands. The grazing of cattle and the drying of cloth have now ceased, but the charm of Heighington remains and it will continue to evoke such remarks as the one attributed to Sir Timothy Eden: 'as sweet a place of rural England as can be found anywhere'.

Heighington station, between Newton Aycliffe and the village, is on the Heritage Line (see Darlington) and has a special place in history. In September 1825 an assortment of engine parts, which had been transported from Newcastle on horse-drawn carts, was re-assembled and placed on the railway line. This was Stephenson's Locomotion Number 1 and it is no surprise to discover that the pub in the former station building is named Locomotion Number 1. In addition to its numerous artefacts of railway nostalgia the locals will confirm that it serves good food.

What, might one ask, have Heighington Level, Old Bolingbroke and countless similar locations in common? They are little-known places where significant happenings of historical importance took place.

Spennymoor

At the junction of the A167 and the A688 six miles south of Durham.

Driving through Spennymoor today you may well wonder how the name 'Thorn Moorland' came to be applied and how free grazing might be accomplished. The answer does indeed 'lie in the soil' or at least under it in the shape of coal and it is within the last 150 years that the transformation took place. In fact, two transformations, for after the coal strike of 1926 the town's fortunes were drastically reduced. Some prosperity did return with the establishing of a Government Ordnance Factory in the district, this going some way to reverse the image of a depressed area. Today, new industrial estates have helped considerably and the siting of the Sedgefield District Council Offices in the town also brought employment, and possibly some confusion.

Even St Paul's church which was established in 1875 suffered a misfortune in the shape of a disastrous fire in 1953. In the immediate surrounds the ecclesiastical picture is completed with St Andrews, Tudhoe Grange, the Roman Catholic church with its vast interior and the usual assortment of Free churches.

Aesthetically speaking the town never really had a chance. Red-bricked Victorian terraces displaying pseudo-classsical styles and, in recent times, towering monstrosities which one writer likens to 'enormous broiler houses' have not helped matters.

On the outskirts of the town are the villages of Byers Green, Tudhoe and Kirk Merrington, from which, with its elevated position, there are extensive views. To a degree these places redress the balance.

To the east across the A167 lies Ferryhill which will be remembered by many for its deep cutting, in the days when travelling the A1 was an adventure – exciting or frustrating depending on your point of view.

The history of the town, which was by-passed by the deep ravine, includes connections with the monastery at Durham and coal mining, as long ago as the twelfth century when its name was simply Ferry. Having driven up the mile long hill on the approach to the town it will not be too difficult to appreciate its present name – Ferryhill.

Bishop Auckland

Eleven miles south of Durham on the A167 and A688.

Since the twelfth century the town has been the seat of the Bishops of Durham, the castle being the residence. It is not open to the public but the chapel is at certain times and the grounds, which contain a well preserved Gothic deercote or house, are very popular with the local population. Originally a Norman manor house, it was converted into a castle around 1300 by Bishop Bek and since that time has undergone a number of changes, the principal one being a Bishop Cosin who restored the building to its former glory. The Bishop also adapted a new chapel from the old hall which again has seen many improvements. The chapel should be visited if possible for it is a lovely place and was re-decorated and re-constructed in 1888, when a conclave of Bishops from overseas attended. This event and the history of Northumbria from Saint Aidan to Saint Cuthbert are depicted in the nine new windows which theologian, Bishop Lightfoot, inserted.

Arriving in the town square from one of the steep ascents from the north one is invited, with a little imagination, to compare it to a French town. The two adjoining buildings which dominate it are the Town Hall and the Victorian church of Saint Anne, which both lend support to the 'French connection'. Two eighteenth century brick houses, Barclays Bank and the Kings Arms also give character to the square. The supermarket, of course, does not and when

Sir John Priestman laid a stone to 'the glory of God' in the former educational institution, he would not know that its ultimate fate would be that of shopping emporium.

The pedestrianisation of much of the square has restricted vehicles, though buses are usually exempt from the restrictions of mere car owners. Will the time come when the driving test will include a section on the understanding of 'no go areas', restricted times, directions, exceptions etc?

The main shopping thoroughfare, Newgate Street, was formerly the Roman route between York and Hadrian's Wall and on it is the Yorkshire Bank building which has more affinity with the buildings in the square. Beyond the shopping precinct and bus station is the white tower which has no architectural significance, it being yet another Government office block – a concrete filing cabinet wherein humans are pigeon-holed.

The ancient mother church of Saint Andrew, or South Church, stands above the River Gaunless just south of the town centre. At 157 feet long it is reputedly the biggest church in the county and a much more imposing building than the one in the square. Fortunately, the charm of its thirteenth century architecture has survived the numerous alterations, particularly in Victorian times. 'Bishop' has a long history of success in the soccer world, its local team having graced the Wembley turf at more than one amateur cup final. Whilst never reaching the exalted heights of north-eastern neighbours Newcastle or Sunderland, its team, much admired in the area, has given pleasure to thousands of supporters.

Leaving the town in a westerly direction towards the two other Aucklands the ribbon development along the road is perhaps best forgotten.

Saint Helen Auckland

On the A688 south-west of Bishop Auckland.

There are two prominent buildings here, the hall and the church. As though offering compensation for the unsightly route into the village, Saint Helen Hall is a pleasant surprise. It is a Palladian house which has an interesting history, not least being the problem of the identity of the architect! Having survived several owners and near complete decay it was eventually restored to its former glory. As if to apologize for its location one is reminded that 'some of the finest palaces in Venice are in the tattiest surroundings'. It is not open to the public.

Next door, so to speak, is the church of Saint Helen – an unusual building which to some degree hides its function. You could be forgiven for passing the sombre fortified exterior and not recognising it. The interior is more inviting and certainly more church like and a connection with the Eden family lies in the gift of the pulpit and lectern which Sybil, mother of Lord Avon, made to it.

Durham's rolling acres. A May evening at Grains o' the Beck, on the road over
the Pennines from Middleton-in-Teesdale to Brough in Cumbria.
(*Geoffrey N. Wright*)

Durham City's great glory is 'the grandest Norman Cathedral in Christendom', perched high above a loop of the river Wear. It is here seen from Palace Green (above) and from river level (right).
(*British Tourist Authority; G. Bernard Wood*)

Durham contrasts.
Above: Panorama across the empty expanses of Upper Weardale.
(*British Tourist Authority*)
Left: Queuing for the tramcar at Beamish, the open-air museum which has
won many awards for its success in recreating the life of yesteryear.
(*British Tourist Authority*)

Causey Arch, near Tanfield, built in 1727 and now reputedly the world's oldest surviving railway bridge. Its builder is said to have killed himself, so worried was he that the structure would collapse!
(*Geoffrey N. Wright*)

Stanhope, 'capital of Weardale' and now a conservation area.
There are fine views of this town from the Barnard Castle to Hexham road.
(*W. R. Mitchell*)

Croft, south of Darlington, is a divided village, the river Tees forming
the boundary between County Durham and North Yorkshire.
The church is on the Yorkshire side.
(*W. R. Mitchell*)

Low Force, where the river Tees presents an exhilarating picture
as it tumbles over an outcrop of whin sill.

West Auckland

On the A688 adjacent to Saint Helen Auckland.

With relief, the ribbon development described perhaps disparagingly comes to an abrupt halt as you enter the village. It is well known as a place for passing through, lying on the A68, the Corbridge road, and the 'back way' to Scotland. The centre of the village is in reality one huge road junction across which the locals appear to have mastered the technique of proceeding. On the north side is the Old Hall, once the home of the Eden family, and now a hotel, whilst across the green on the south side the only building of merit is a seventeenth century house with mullioned windows and decorative porch. Readers of family histories will find a veritable array of talent in the Eden family, including MPs (one a Prime Minister), bishops, generals, an admiral and a distinguished author. This latter, Sir Timothy, has written what is generally acclaimed the best of the books on Durham. It is in the County Book series.

Escomb Church

North of the A6073 between Bishop Auckland and High Etherley.

Within the confines of this book it would not be possible to list all the churches which are thought to be of interest. Escomb lies at the opposite end of the spectrum to Durham, but linked with the common purpose for which they are built. It is perhaps the most mysterious of the churches in that its history is not recorded with any accuracy, and its survival due in part to its obscurity. The most reasonable date is around 670AD and whilst the excellent coloured booklet explains it all you are asked to first explore the church both inside and out before reading it.

That over worked word 'incongruous' certainly applies to Escomb and it is something of a surprise to discover this jewel, not 'set in a silver sea' but surrounded by a council estate at the end of the village. The key can be obtained from Number 23, this being the age of the locked church. Do make your way to it, particularly if a feeling for the historical appeals to you, but do not be confused by a large churchyard as you enter the village. The church is at the far end by the Post Office.

Witton

To the west of Bishop Auckland encircled by the A68, the A6073 and the A689

Being but a 'stone's throw' from Shildon, it is no surprise to learn that the first railway was laid from the colliery in these parts. Sadly there appears to be no official recognition of this fact and when you light upon the actual site at Phoenix Row, a kindly resident will indicate its beginnings. Phoenix Row is reached by turning left along The Baltic by the Royal Hotel at Witton Park. Pass the Methodist church and the house dated 1854, then round the back to seek out the former track now a walkway to West Auckland and Shildon.

Witton Castle dates from before 1410 when the former manor house was fortified. Today it is the focal point of a leisure complex – camping, caravanning, banqueting and trade fares.

The village of Witton le Wear stands on a wooded hill above the river and on the A68. It contrasts sharply with the industrialised village of Witton Park and its location on rising ground has enhanced its character.

Crook

At the junction of the A689 from Bishop Auckland and the A690 from Durham.

Since the demise of the old collieries and the arrival of new industries the town has received a face-lift and the centre is quite smart with a not unpleasant blend of old and new. The oldest feature, decorative rather than utilitarian, is the Devil's Stone, a volcanic type rock probably transported from distant Borrowdale during the great Ice Age. Close by is the town's War Memorial. The nineteenth century parish church of Saint Catherine is at the lower end of the large green and behind it on higher ground the Roman Catholic church with its imposing tower. Crook has been dubbed 'the gateway to Weardale' and since millions of pounds were spent on reclamation work this might now be justified. What was once the very first commercial coke plant in England at nearby Roddymoor now has sheep and cattle grazing on it. A little to the north are two of the euphemistically name pit villages of Durham – Billy Row and Mount Pleasant.

Shildon

South of Bishop Auckland on the A6072.

The town of Shildon is synonymous with railway history, but alas today the workshops are no more and the consequential air of depression pervades the town. A life line in the shape of an active development agency offers a ray of hope and new industries are very much in evidence. Even an old school building has found a new lease of life. It has to be said that the town does not exactly encourage the tourist to explore it, even when the industrial heritage is so marked and interesting. To compare it, as a tourist attraction, with say Barnard Castle would be most unfair and yet its place in the history of transport cannot be denied.

If the name Timothy Hackworth does not immediately ring a bell it will be because he was overshadowed by his contemporary, George Stephenson. A visit to the excellent museum complex at Soho House and nearby buildings will reveal the fascinating story of the birth of the railway. 'Sans Pareil' – without equal – is a replica of the locomotive which competed in the Rainhill Trials of 1829 against the better remembered 'Rocket'. This replica actually featured in the anniversary celebrations – also at Rainhill. When the Queen Mother opened the renovated complex in 1975 to coincide with the 150th anniversary of the Stockton and Darlington railway, it was awarded a 'Come to Britain' tourist trophy.

One of the the three rail trails follows the line of the old railway and after Brussleton continues to Phoenix Row which is mentioned above under Witton. The booklet which describes them in detail has some interesting facts about the town and about Hackworth.

Also in the town is the world's first ticket office, Coach House, and a plaque on the wall confirms this. Adamson, who was the Landlord of the Grey Mare, had connections with the Daniel Adamson, boiler makers, now in Dukinfield, Greater Manchester.

On the outskirts of the town is the comprehensive school and the Sunnydale Leisure Centre – on the same site and an example of how an enlightened authority encourages the two to work together for their mutual benefit.

On a completely different historical tack, Robert Lilburne, one of the signatories to the death warrant of Charles I, came from East Tickley, and at Middridge Grange lived Colonel Anthony Byerley who supported the king. A veritable example in the same town of 'for and against'.

Do go to Shildon – there is something very special about a plaque which informs that: 'From Shildon, near this site, the Stockton and Darlington Railway Company on 27 September 1825 ran the first passenger train drawn by a steam engine'.

Tow Law

On the A68 seven miles south of Consett.

Literally astride the A68, Tow Law is a place for passing through quickly. This is not meant disrespectfully, but simply that it is a cold bleak place as well it might be with an elevation of just over 1,000 feet and totally exposed to the elements. The villagers seem not to be too put out by its location and in days past the local football team earned a coveted tag – 'Giant Killers'. Today's team in the Northern League enjoys a faithful following. The ground is opposite Bond Foundry Company, one of the few employers in the area. In summer the busiest place on Tuesdays and Thursdays is the popular cattle market and currently there is much activity on open cast mining sites. Restoration work is in hand and if it is modelled on other sites in the county it will be much appreciated.

The church of Saint Phillip and Saint James stands rather forlornly by the old railway station and old foundry. From 1888 to 1934 its incumbent was amateur astronomer, Thomas Espin, who had an observatory in the vicarage garden.

In their heyday the furnaces, which made cannon balls for the Crimean War, and the mines in the area employed nearly 2,000 men. But times change and so too does the naming of offspring. An examination of gravestones will reveal that males had such Biblical names as Ezekial, Zacharia, Matthew and Luke.

Wolsingham

On the A689 six miles west of Crook and eleven miles from Bishop Auckland.

If the approach to a town or village is likely to colour your image of the place then you should make your way to Wolsingham via Hamsterley village and forest (see page 60). Travelling direct from Bishop Auckland on the A689 your first 'landmark' - if that is the word - is the steel works or, more correctly, Wolsingham Steel Limited - British Shipbuilders - Engineering Division. The village can be justly proud of the company since it provides employment and in the maritime world it 'has a long tradition of service to the Royal and Merchant Navies'. In the wider field of industry the company specialises in heavy steel castings for most sections of engineering.

The village itself, though busy with passing traffic, has a number of interesting attractions and they are listed in the Walkabout pamphlet. This is Number 5 in the Durham County Council series and these handy guides will assist you in your exploration of the county.

Within the space of an hour and walking less than a mile you can appreciate Wolsingham's place in the history of the dale. You will not be surprised to learn that it had an abundance of taverns and there is an interesting game which can be played in most market towns. 'Which of the private houses were once inns?'

Patients will have no difficulty in recognising the former Golden Lion - it is now the doctor's surgery. The finest buildings in Wolsingham are Whitfield Cottages which were originally - yes you've guessed it - an inn. This was the Packhorse complete with stables at the rear. Next door is a much larger building, Whitfield House, built in 1700 and thought by some to be not in keeping with the rest of the town. The trees which front the house are a rare Mediterranean species - evergreen holm oaks.

Opposite the old Bank House is Church Lane and two interesting buildings are passed en route to the church of Saint Mary and Saint Stephen, which is itself a fine Regency structure. The first is Padua House which has examples of blocked windows and the second, the Masonic Hall, was once the grammar school in which the thumb screw helped to maintain discipline in the 1870s.

North of the town is a picnic area at Demesne Mill and still higher on the Lanchester Road is Redgate Cross, a memorial to religious intolerance and reached by a flight of stone steps. The inscription reads: 'Near this spot Venerable John Duckett was arrested. He was afterwards tried at Sunderland and taken to Tyburn where he was executed for being a priest, September 7 1644'.

It is from this vantage point that you will have far reaching views of Weardale, and, of course, the town below you.

Stanhope

On the A689 twelve miles west of Crook and seventeen miles from Bishop Auckland.

If you are following the 'roller-coaster' route on the B6278 between Barnard Castle and Hexham you will see all Stanhope lying below you as you descend Crawleyside from the north or Catterick Moss from the south. At river level you can ford the Wear quite safely if it is not running too high or too swift. Adventurous offspring can cross by the stepping stones as you splash through to the far bank, though a more convenient bridge is available if you are hesitant.

Again, a Walkabout pamphlet is available for Stanhope, and after the delights of the river the centre piece, so to speak, is the fossil tree stump. This lies to the west of the gate to the church of Saint Thomas; it is thought to be 250 million years old and was found on the moors near Edmundbyers Cross. The church, built around 1200, has some fine examples of local Frosterley marble and to their credit the stonemasons of the mid nineteenth century used the original stone when the aisles were extended. In spring a colourful array of daffodils borders the path from the gate to the porch.

The mock medieval castle built in 1798 might now be something of an embarrassment though at the time it was no doubt much revered by the Gateshead MP who built it in spite of it making him bankrupt. It was in more recent times a reform school.

Other buildings of note in Stanhope are Horn Hall, Newtown House, Unthank Hall, Bulls House, Stone House and Stanhope Hall. This latter is thought to be the most imposing building in the dale and is a fortified manor house dating from the mid twelfth century. It is part medieval, part Elizabethan and part Jacobean, having remained in the same family until 1704 when the last male fell at Blenheim. In the Dene, past the hall, is evidence of lead and ironstone mining with the attendant paraphernalia of smelting mills, furnaces and kilns. As we shall see later, the search today is for fluorspar. Unthank Hall has an interesting derivation - the word meaning 'without leave' which suggests that squatters are no respectors of style, this being an Elizabethan farmhouse.

Stanhope is dubbed 'capital of Weardale', and today it is a conservation area.

A little to the east is Frosterley where the famous marble was once extensively quarried. This is not the case now and winning it appears very much a hit and miss affair, whilst the industrial activity is centred on the plant which processes the fluorspar mined further up the dale.

Travelling westwards up the dale you will pass through Eastgate, Westgate, and Daddry Shield before reaching St John's Chapel. There are two points of interest at Eastgate: the road goes up right to Rookhope, the location of Sir Walter Scott's poem, 'Harold the Dauntless', then continues to Allenheads, and the second feature is the cement works which you cannot fail to observe. If you know the beautiful Hope Valley in Derbyshire and recognise the Blue Circle you will know that once again fate has decreed that this essential ingredient for building is found in some of England's most scenic places. At Westgate the Bishop of Durham no longer has a residence but the village does boast a ski slope on Swinhope Moor. The red brick houses look somewhat out of step with the more natural stone but the presence of the river as it tumbles along could divert your attention from this architectural blunder. You are now very much into sheep farming country as you follow the Wear towards Daddry Shield where you cross it as you run onto St John's Chapel.

St John's Chapel
On the A689 eight miles west of Stanhope
Why this Weardale village was thus named is so obvious it seems hardly necessary to confirm that a chapel built in 1465 was the reason. It was subsequently replaced, in the late 1700s, by the Georgian building which is today's church.

If you climb Chapel Fell, the minor road south to Langdon Beck, you will, at 2,000 feet, be travelling on what is generally thought to be England's highest highway. You will not be surprised to discover that by the quarries at the summit the view of Weardale is breathtaking. Ask in the village for directions to the waterfall at nearby Harthope Burn which is one of the natural attractions of the area. A caravan park behind the main street and the Rancho del Rio nightspot complete the picture before moving into even wilder country.

Head of Weardale
The A689 Alston road
The countryside becomes bleaker and the population more sparse as you proceed from St John's Chapel to the county boundary just before reaching Nenthead. The next hamlet is Ireshopeburn which, as you will appreciate when you see its location, is very popular with hill walkers. A popular local walk leads to Burnhope Reservoir which can also be reached by car making a diversion to Cowshill. John Wesley's visit to miners and farmers in 1749 is commemorated with a plaque.

KILHOPE WHEEL.

At Cowshill a minor road right, the B6295, runs north to Allenheads and Allendale Town which are in Northumberland. Staying on the Alston road you are entering very bleak North Pennine country and after Lanehead there is patchy forestation, the dark green squares like some giant moorland quilt.

Killhope Wheel is suddenly upon you on your left and to reach it you follow the signs across the burn and onto the car park. The story of lead mining is very clearly portrayed in a static exhibition and slide show at the complex and even the person who professes to have no knowledge of or interest in the subject will not fail to be impressed. A Community Task Force, much in evidence in such places, has been busy on restoration work at Killhope and anyone interested in industrial archaeology would find a great deal to occupy them here.

Just a piece up the road from the Wheel and you leave Durham for Cumbria and that most isolated of market towns, Alston.

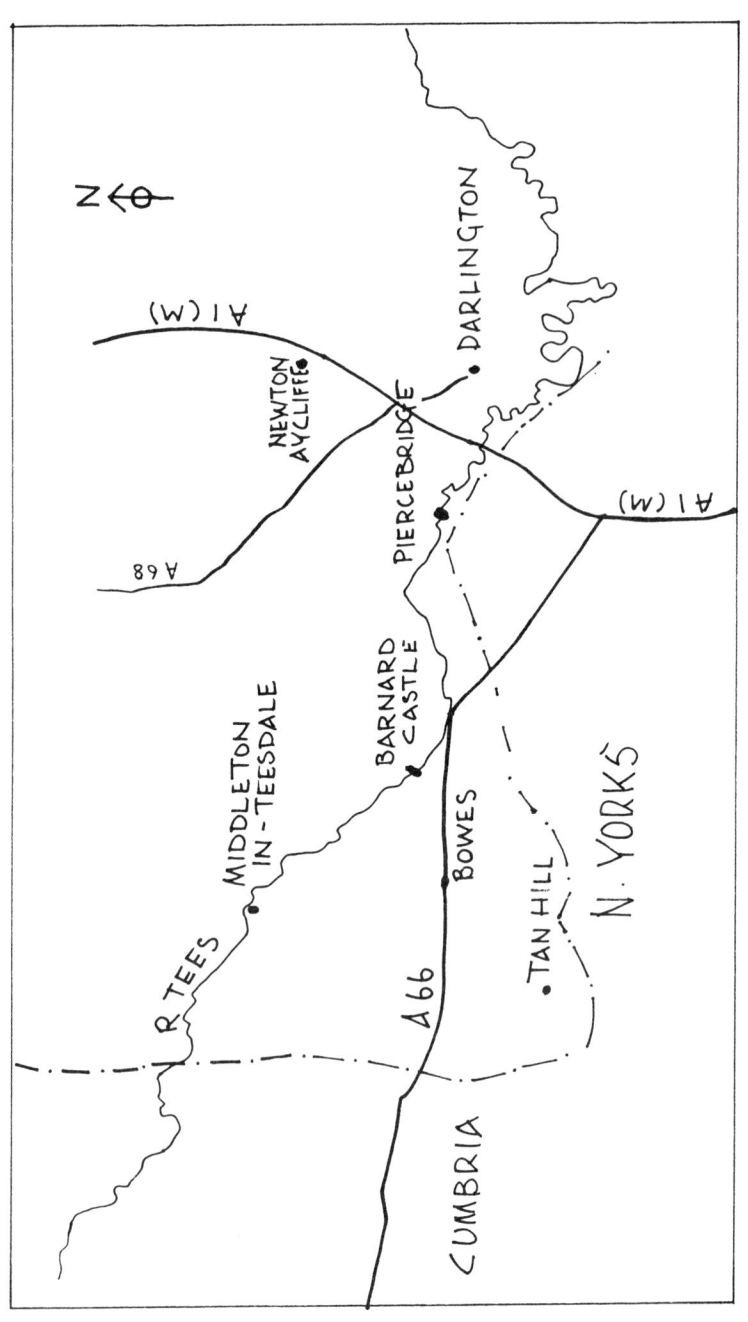

C. Teesdale

The dales of the Tees and the Wear have much in common and both are popular with tourists but they also have striking differences, particularly in the matter of industry. Teesdale has not been exploited for mineral wealth after the manner of Weardale and consequently the whole area has a more natural aspect - an unspoilt countryside. There are signs of former stone quarries and lead mines which date from Roman times, but they do not offend the eye to any degree.

Barnard Castle is the accepted 'gateway' town and it is both historic, with its ancient castle, and artistic with its 'Taj Mahal' of the north-east - the Bowes Museum. To motor up the dale through Cotherstone, Romaldkirk and Middleton is an extremely pleasant exercise with equally pleasant rewards in the tumbling waters of the river and the rugged scenery.

As with most rural communities Teesdale has its quota of events including the grand Spring Holiday Meet weekend at Barnard Castle, the village agricultural and horticultural shows and, of course, the inevitable carnival. The area is particularly appealing to the outdoor pursuit individual with the Pennine Way much in evidence and passing England's highest waterfall, High Force. Angling, sailing, water and winter skiing, pony trekking and golf are also available in the dale. If you are new to the area a guided walk might be of interest and there are a number available during the summer months. Travelling en route to Scotland and escaping from motorway madness you may have come across Teesdale quite by accident. Having discovered it, call again and stay longer to enjoy its lovely scenery.

Both Scott and Dickens found inspiration for their writing which suggests a certain magic about the place. Before touring the dale proper there are three villages, Staindrop, Gainford and Piercebridge, which should be visited.

Staindrop
On the A688 eight miles south-west of Bishop Auckland
The village is best known for its association with Raby Castle which is on its northern side. It dates from King Canute's reign but it was in the fourteenth century that the Nevilles fortified and generally improved what is thought to be one of England's finest castles. In the mid sixteenth century the Nevilles were disgraced through their association with the abortive attempt to overthrow Elizabeth I. In 1626 Sir Henry Vane purchased Raby and Barnard castles for the seemingly 'bargain price' of £18,000 and so it remains today in the same family, being the seat of Lord Barnard.

The castle is set in beautiful rolling parklands and its attractions include a medieval kitchen, rare paintings and numerous rooms of exquisite delight. To wander through the walled garden to the deer park after visiting the carriage collection in the stables is a most rewarding exercise. On leaving the castle, do pause in the village to visit the parish church of Saint Mary. Originally dedicated to Saint Gregory, it is of Saxon foundation and though obviously added to, even as recent as the eighteenth century, the Saxon influence is still very evident. There are memorials and hatchments to both the Neville and the Vane families.

Within the space of half an hour one can walk along Staindrop's main street, Front Street and Office Square, and view several buildings of character: the sixteenth century manor house, the Georgian estates office, the seventeenth century Gorst Hall, the eighteenth century Westfield House, the fanlight of Ebor House, the old blacksmith's shop, the incongruous red-bricked Malvern House, and finally, Staindrop Hall and Staindrop House -a veritable assortment of architectural styles.

There is an American connection at nearby Cockfield village where Jeremiah Dixon was born. His name is associated with the controversial Mason-Dixon line.

Gainford

On the A67 eight miles west of Darlington.

Gainford is mercifully just off the busy A67 and one has to know where to turn off left to the Cross Keys to view this quiet backwater. It is yet another of Durham's 'green' villages - this time quite a sizeable sward as distinct from other villages which boast a number of smaller greens. It is bordered by graceful Georgian houses but some blunder in the planning department has permitted the building of 'town houses' not in keeping with the existing architectural styles.

Being so enclosed, originally for defensive purposes against the marauding Scots, the village was quite self-sufficient. Time was when bootmakers, blacksmiths, tailors and the like served a population of a mere 700, but the coming of the railway and better roads saw the role of the village change to that of dormitory for commuters.

From one central point by the column to mark Queen Victoria's sixtieth reign, it is possible to see all that is best in Gainford and the walkabout leaflet will describe in some detail the various attractions.

The church of Saint Mary was built in the thirteenth century using earlier stone from the Roman fort at Piercebridge and confirmation of this was given in 1864 when a Roman altar was discovered. Houses of note include the former Saint Colette's Schoolhouse, the Georgian West House, the Bank and Westmorland House, the eighteenth century terrace High Row and the mansion house, the end of the High Row and to the left is Gainford Hall. This is a Jacobean mansion and, considering its ruinous condition a hundred years ago, it is now a fine building which together with the seventeenth century dovecote is listed. Neither are open to the public but can be viewed from outside.

The attempt to promote Gainford as a spa was short livied, but its role as a typical English village has changed little. When the Hatfield survey of 1375 described the place as, 'a thriving hamlet, not molested or perturbed by the King's enemies' it was hardly envisaged that it would apply to the scene today. Do search it out and view it closely.

Piercebridge
On the A67 five miles west of Darlington and on Roman Dere Street.

The peace of this lovely spot is almost shattered by the traffic on the busy A67 which does in fact now by-pass it. Lying astride the Tees it is on the Durham/ Yorkshire border with most of the village being in Durham. Piercebridge is noted for its Roman fort which is very well preserved and a popular spot for those on the Roman Britain trail. It has open greens and a lovely stretch of the Tees crossed by a three-arched stone bridge. Architecturally it does not compare with say, Gainford, but the cream and white-washed cottages which border the green do present a pictorial scene worth recording on film. The oldest house in Piercebridge stands next to Saint Mary's church and the third century Roman fort is located behind the cottages on the south side of the green. Objects from the fort can be seen both in the Bowes Museum and in the British Museum.

Barnard Castle
At the junction of the A688 from Bishop Auckland and the A67 sixteen miles west of Darlington.

The architectural attractions of the town are the Market Cross, the Bowes Museum and the castle, but this latter is not easily seen, it being tucked out of the way on the road out west. It is a Norman building begun by Bernard Balliol, who gave his name to the town, and it was subsequently added to until in 1629 it was dismantled by Sir Henry Vane in whose family it remained until 1952 when it was presented to the nation.

The best view of the castle is obtained from The Bridge which itself has a colourful history, it being the Gretna Green of the district where illicit weddings were conducted for half a crown by a Bible clerk, one Cuthbert Hilton. During the castle siege of 1569 The Bridge was damaged and major re-building took place, but it was much later, in the eighteenth and nineteenth centuries, that the curious squinch arches were added. These can be seen on the town bank side and were designed to give extra strength to The Bridge.

Before climbing back into the town you will notice the site of the old Ullathornes Mill which in its day was one of the largest shoe-thread factories in Britain. Beyond Flax Field and running off the Middleton Road, a footbridge crosses the Tees into Flatts Wood. Walking back along The Stills, the west bank of the river, you can cross by another footbridge and approach the town via Thorngate and The Bank. You will pass sixteenth and eighteenth century houses as you climb to the ornate Market Cross, the focal point of the market place. Built in 1747 it has served as the Town Hall, a lockup and a market for dairy produce. The weather vane served as a target when two local marksmen fired their muskets to settle a debt.

The grandest street in 'Barney' is the graceful curve of the Market Place which continues as the Horse Market. There are four buildings of note - the hostelries, the Kings Head and the Golden Lion, Witham Hall which houses the library and the imposing Methodist church at the junction with Galgate. A number of alleys and courtyards run off the main thoroughfare and, though the commercialisation of certain properties is apparent, there is still evidence of former architectural styles. From 'the square' Galgate runs in a north-easterly direction towards Bishop Auckland and on it is one of the town's oldest buldings, the Three Horseshoes Hotel, dating from 1691. Murchison House is a dignified three-storey building, the former home of Sir Roderick Murchison who, as President of the Royal Geographical Society, achieved fame for his expeditioin to the Nile and Lake Victoria. Numbers 57 to 59A form a building known as The Grove which was built by historian W E Hutchinson who concluded that Galgate was formerly Gallowgate and before that Hangslave, the site of the town's gallows. The other prominent structure at this point is the Boer War memorial.

BARNARD CASTLE

44

Return now to the Market Cross and Newgate where stands the parish church of Saint Mary which though Norman in origin was much restored in the nineteenth century. It contains a lot to interest the visitor as too does its surrounds, the churchyard. Here a stone cross by an avenue of lime trees commemorates the death of 143 townsfolk who died of Asiatic cholera in 1849.

A little along Newgate stands the Roman Catholic church and just beyond that is the jewel of the town, the Bowes Museum. Built by a French architect after the manner of a French chateau it was to house the fine collection of John Bowes, a leading coal owner and son of the tenth Earl of Strathmore. It is now in the care of Durham County Council and amongst its treasures which include furniture, porcelain and tapestries are paintings by El Greco and Goya.

By the time it was opened in 1892 both the founder and his French wife, Josephine, had been dead for some time. The Bowes Museum has to be included on any list of 'places to visit' and it is perhaps not without significance that so fine a building should have been built by someone whose wealth was obtained from an industry which so disfigured the landscape.

'Barney' is indeed the gateway to Teesdale and, equipped with the appropriate walkabout leaflets, you will embark on a journey full of interest.

Eggleston Abbey is on a minor road running from the Museum towards Greta Bridge and in the area of the confluence of the Greta and the Tees. It is an example of a premonstratensian abbey and is in a picturesque location.

Romaldkirk

On the B6277 six miles north-west of Barnard Castle.

From Barnard Castle to Middleton in Teesdale there are two routes - the direct one north of the river and via Eggleston and the prettier drive from the castle along the B6277 via Lartington and Cotherstone. A diversion left to Hury Reservoir takes you into Baldersdale before returning you to Hunderthwaite and Romaldkirk. There are, in fact, a number of diversions into the hills to view several reservoirs in these parts and they are well signed.

Romaldkirk is an ancient village and a favourite watering place for tourists. Its architectural style gives away its true location, for it is in reality a North Riding of Yorkshire village, only lately 'transferred' by a quirk of the administration. There is no symmetrical pattern about the various greens and the location of the houses which border them. This apparent haphazard planning has given the place its character and the numerous surprise views one gets when walking about. The name comes from the short-lived infant son of a Northumberland king who, though only three days old when he died, became the patron saint of Buckingham where his mother had fled to bear the child.

The church dates from Saxon times, though much of its present structure is of twelfth and fifteenth centuries, and a handy guide to the village is available inside. The Rose and Crown is the centre of attraction with good food, ale and conversation which has been known to dwell on the matter of where true loyalties lie - Yorkshire or Durham.

A back way round the Church leads to the seventeenth century almshouses built by William Hutchinson of London and restored in 1829. As you motor on towards Middleton in Teesdale you will notice across to your left the track of the former railway.

Middleton in Teesdale

On the B6277 ten miles from Barnard Castle.

Approaching this popular centre on a Friday might alarm you as the rapid patter of the cattle market auctioneer pervades the whole village. This is obviously an important farming centre and if you can avoid getting under feet or parking carelessly you should experience this event.

Your first call might well be the Tourist Information Centre which has a most helpful staff who will ensure you derive the greatest benefit from your visit. Middleton was a busy lead mining centre and the imposing Bainbridge Memorial Fountain serves as a tribute to the London Lead Company's manager. After the fashion of a coal mining village, nine out of ten people in the area were connected with the lead industry and its development was of a 'company' town absorbing a small rural village, much of this activity taking place in the mid 1800s.

Strangely, the Quaker owners of the company didn't establish a Friends' Meeting House, though most other denominations are represented, and one former Methodist chapel is now a listed building.

The story of Middleton is so closely related to the history of the Lead Company that one wonders what form the old village would have taken had the mineral not been so evident in these parts. Architecturally, it does not have the variety often found elsewhere, but what it does have is worth viewing. For instance, the separate belfry of Saint Mary's church is unique in Durham, the original bells being bequeathed by none other than Parson William Bell! If you are familiar with the bell cage at East Bergholt in Suffolk you will be equally interested in Saint Mary's.

There is a 'yesteryear' atmosphere in the town guide which describes the former police station, former Baptist chapel, former Company school, former Primitive Methodist chapel, former cornmill and the former Superintendent's abode - Middleton House.

Flanagan and Allen would have been at home in Middleton where 'underneath the arches' has more than a musical connotation. Starting at the approach to New Town where you pass under an ornamental arch, there are some thirty or more in and around the town including the single arch of County Bridge. Historians would have little difficulty in determining the relationship between housing and class structure. The terraced cottages for the lower strata and the larger houses with stables for under managers and professional people reflect the system. Tap housings, where a common water supply was available, were a common feature and can still be seen. In the days of self-sufficiency each house would have its own vegetable patch and a pig sty and one or two examples of these are still to be found.

Whilst not aspiring to an arboretum the town does have an interesting variety of trees: a monkey-puzzle tree (Chilean pine) and a weeping ash, as distinct from a willow, can be found beyond the Market Cross. In the parkland the Wellingtonia or giant redwood will not reach the dizzy height, 365 feet, of its Californian cousin, but will probaby settle for a mere 100. Like most popular country towns Middleton has an influx of tourists during the summer, most of whom are en route to the numerous attractions in the area. They would do well to pause a while longer and look closer at a town which probably has no equal, certainly not in Durham.

Low Force and Bowlees Visitor Centre

On the B6277 three miles from Middleton in Teesdale.

The tumbling Tees presents an exhilarating picture at both High and Low Force and a visit first to the excellent Bowlees Visitor Centre will point you in the right direction. This former chapel now houses an exhibition on the geological and historical aspects of the area and the adjacent picnic site is a good base from which to view Gibson's Cave, Summerhill Force, Wynch Bridge and Low Force. Walk on past the toilet block to Gibson's Cave, over which flows Summerhill Force, a most scenic ten minute stroll which will be equalled but not often surpassed in many places. This is reminiscent of Hardraw Force, near Hawes, except that brass band concerts are not likely to be held here. The adventurous will go behind the water for that spectacular photograph but only with extreme care.

Back at the car park do spend a little time in the Visitor Centre before making your way across the road, through the kissing gate and two fields, to Wynch Bridge. The original suspension footbridge erected by lead miners was reputed to be England's oldest and in 1802 one of the eleven persons on it was killed when the bridge broke. Today you are advised that one person at a time should cross, though not all who do will be following the finger post - 'Pennine Way'. Most will be admiring the Tees as it tumbles over the rocks on its way to the sea at Middlesbrough.

High Force and Cauldron Snout

On the B6277 just beyond Bowlees: Cauldron Snout is south of the new Cow Green Reservoir which is west of Forest in Teesdale.

High Force is England's highest waterfall, the Tees falling seventy feet over Great Whin Sill, though less forceful since the building of Cow Green

Reservoir. It is reached by walking down the woodland path opposite the High Force Hotel and is part of the Raby Estate. So long as you are in the area it is a pity not to see it, particularly when the river is running fairly deep.

After High Force is Forest-in-Teesdale to which youngsters were evacuated during World War II, no doubt believing that this was the other side of the world! The next junction is Langdon Beck where the highest main road in England runs north over Langdon Common to St John's Chapel in Weardale. The road left and due west from Langdon Beck runs on to Cow Green Reservoir where you may park to walk on to Cauldron Snout. This is the longest and largest cataract in England, a 200 hundred foot cascade over dolerite rocks.

By a disused mine on the edge of Widdybank Fell is 'the Isle of Man' but you are hardly likely to be troubled by TT motor cyclists in these parts. This minor road from Langdon will take you back to the B6277, then on via Garrigill to Alston. If you are not familiar with this elevated Cumbrian market town you might run on and visit it since you are so near. Should you be leaving Durham and heading north after your visit to Teesdale, then either Alston and Penrith, or Weardale, Allendale and Hexham could well be alternative scenic routes for you to explore.

HIGH FORCE

Bowes

On the A66 at the junction with the A688 four miles from Barnard Castle and fifteen from Scotch Corner.

Originally in Yorkshire when the Tees formed the boundary, but annexed to Durham at the 1974 shuffle, Bowes has a number of interesting 'connections'. The Queen Mother's family is connected to the original Bowes - William de Arcubus who commanded the Norman castle. The much earlier Roman fort was built to defend Stainmoor and Roman remains can be seen in St Giles church whilst in the churchyard are gravestones of the Dickens 'characters'. The nineteen year old George Taylor was the Smike of 'Nicholas Nickleby' whilst headmaster William Shaw was Dickens' model for the notorious Squeers. Dotheboys Hall stands at the west end of the village and the ancient Unicorn where Dickens supped is still offering refreshment to the traveller. A by-pass mercifully allows the village to retain its character. Do not make the mistake, as some have, of going to Bowes to visit the famous Museum. That is at Barnard Castle.

Tan Hill

On a minor road from Reeth, North Yorkshire, up Arkengarthdale.

Dubbed as England's highest inn and featured very prominently in the double-glazing commercials, Tan Hill is a very exposed and isolated hostelry. Its namesake, the 1,732 foot hill, is just over the border in Yorkshire, but the inn itself lies in Durham and close to one of those 'Three Shires Head' locations, the other being Cumbria. If you like getting away from the madding crowd then Tan Hill is for you. By completing the circuit of this mountainous minor road you would find yourself in Keld at the head of Swaledale.

D. East of the Durham Motorway

This section covers all that is left of Durham between the coast and the A1(M) taking in Darlington and the wiggly bits bordering the Tees - also Sedgefield, Peterlee and some famous colliery names like Easington.

There is not a lot to be said about Durham's coastline. Since local government reorganisation, the best bits appear to have been lost to Tyne and Wear in the north and Cleveland in the south. What is left suffers from the pollution associated with coal so that with the exception of Crimdon Beck above Hartlepool and perhaps Seaham, just below Ryehope, one is not exactly encouraged to walk the shore.

This might well be termed the 'bread and butter' area of the county with its largest town, Darlington, its industrial acres around Peterlee, and the long established collieries all contributing to the economy. The graceful Penshaw Monument dominates much of the skyline and a network of goods roads make the rapid transporting of goods so much simpler. The A19 trunk road is the main artery, running north and south and parallel to the A1(M) which is some nine miles to its west. At Sedgefield the horses jump over the sticks on the only racecourse left in the county and the local country park is a popular oasis.

If you haven't seen coal being mined at the coal-face and are not likely to, then put on your wellies and walk the shore-line at Horden. There you will see coal being harvested from the sea. Whilst you are getting the sea air at Seaham, chat to one of the local fishermen about the changes in the harbour system and particularly the financial implications.

Is there friendly rivalry in Croft where the Tees divides the village in two camps - Yorkshire and Durham? And what of Wordsworth - did he find daffodils in Dorset and Durham as well as that famous host in the Lake District?

This may not be the prettiest part of Durham but then, neither is London the most scenic part of Britain. On the other hand, if social and industrial history is your interest, you will find much to occupy your mind.

Darlington

To the east of the A1(M) twenty miles south of Durham.

This is the county's largest town and it has, since 1825 been known as the railway town when the world's first steam-worked public line, the Stockton and Darlington Railway, was inaugurated. The railway connection remains quite strong and the original Locomotion Number 1 stands at Darlington North Road Station Museum, together with other memorabilia of the age.

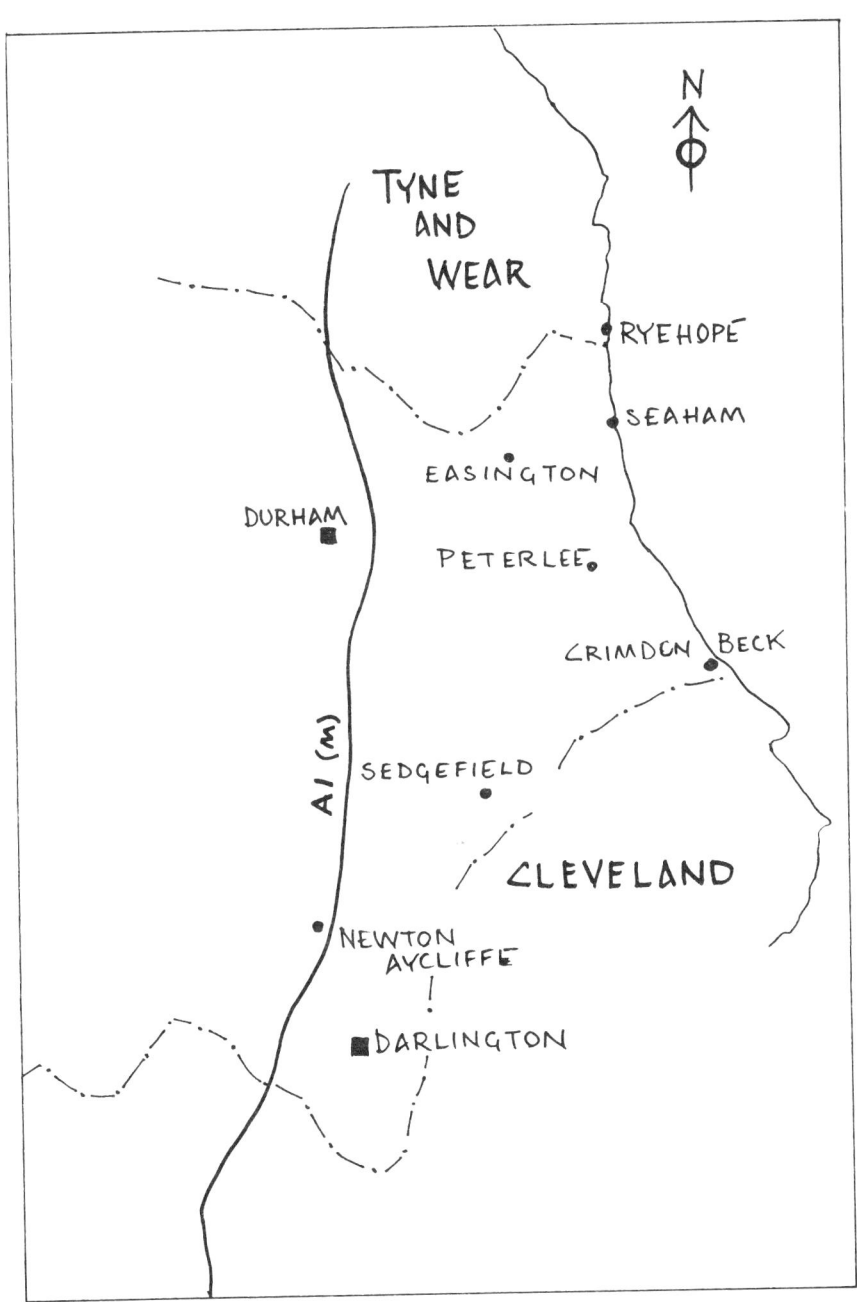

N

TYNE
AND
WEAR

RYEHOPE

SEAHAM

EASINGTON

DURHAM

PETERLEE

CRIMDON BECK

A1 (m)

SEDGEFIELD

CLEVELAND

NEWTON
AYCLIFFE

DARLINGTON

Travellers alighting at Darlington's Bank Top Station will recall that both 'Locomotion' and 'Derwent' were displayed on the platform until 1975 when they were moved to form the major exhibits at the museum. North Road was the original Darlington station when it opened in 1842 and its former lines included one west to Kirkby Stephen and beyond. Today it is on the Heritage Line which runs to Bishop Auckland with connections to Stanhope in Weardale by bus service. Special charter trains are occasionally run over the line into Weardale proper. An explanatory leaflet which has associations with David Bellamy highlights the attractions of the route.

On the same site and therefore somewhat puzzling are the workshops of the Darlington Railway Preservation Society, a charitable body quite separate from the railway museum. Their engines are in a state of repair and an enthusiastic band of volunteers work extremely hard to 'make Darlington more actively conscious of its unique heritage and advertise it to the world'.

The town's museum in Tubwell Row contains exhibits of an archaeological, social and historical nature and in summer there is the added attraction of an observation beehive. Another historical and mechanical marvel is the steam-driven beam pumping engine at the Tees Cottage Pumping Station off the A67, a mile from the town. The engine is on the site of the former waterworks. There is also a rare gas engine of pre World War I vintage (see also Ryehope in this section).

The impressive Saint Cuthburt's church was the 'swan song' of Bishop Pudsey, it being his last and his finest building completed in the late twelfth century. Among its many treasures are Saxon Crosses, a Danish tomb, fifteenth century carved stalls, a pillar which leans at an alarming angle and a comparatively recent, 1865, pulpit by Gilbert Scott. What was Westminster Abbey's loss was Saint Cuthburt's gain in the shape of a mosaic reredos featuring the Last Supper.

The town centre comprises the High Row with its Victorian Market Hall and old Town Hall and an impressive clock tower, a gift of Joseph Pease, one of the town's former MPs. The Pease family played an important role in the developoment of the town as a railway centre and it is John's statue on the High Row.

The passages or ginnels off Skinnergate are known locally as wynds. In the nineteenth century there was a hundred or so of these wynds or yards, many of which contained workers' cottages. Today only a few remain. The two prominent Quaker families of Pease and Backhouse were responsible for some fine examples of architectural styles in the town. What they would have thought of the modern concrete blocks with the obligatory car parks is not for our contemplation.

The town is well blessed with leisure amenities, and the Dolphin Centre on Horsemarket must surely be as complete as one would find anywhere in Britain. With four swimming pools, multi-purpose halls, squash and sauna available, it is no surprise to learn that international sporting tournaments are held there. An indoor bowling centre, two more sports centres and the usual outdoor facilities in the park complete the town picture. The golf courses, as one would expect, are out of the town at Stressholme (municipal), and at Harrowgate Hill, Blackwell and Low Dinsdale.

For theatregoers the Civic Theatre in Parkgate has retained its Edwardian character, whilst the more modern ABC Cinema in Northgate has the now common-place three screens.

Darlington is a fine base from which the surrounding countryside can be explored and the Tees makes a useful reference point. Crossing the river and straying into North Yorkshire will take you to such delights as Richmond, Swaledale and Wensleydale, but for now we will continue to explore Durham County. As though to confirm an earlier assertion, the local guide offers Darlington as the gateway to Northumbria's magnificent coast.

Croft and Hurworth

On the A167 four miles south of Darlington.

Croft is a divided village, the Tees being the boundary between North Yorkshire and County Durham. On the Yorkshire side there is a Lewis Carroll connection in the parish church, whilst the Durham half boasts Saint Cuthbert's Hospital. The river at this point has become much calmer and certainly more meandering which makes exploring the area a pleasant task. Croft and Hurworth mingle together and in the latter village there is a history of a cholera epidemic with bodies being buried on the village green. In the doctor's surgery are old photographs of how life was lived in the past and since many of the patients are of an older generation this must make visiting the doctor's a nostalgic experience.

Hurworth is one of Durham's lineal villages with attractive eighteenth and nineteenth century houses facing each other across a central green. It is built on a ridge on the north bank of the river and it is fortunate in not having been 'developed' and thus retains its character.

Neasham, the next village, has the majority of its houses on one side only and a glance at the local information board will explain why. Flooding was a frequent occurrence before the high bank was built, and 1771 saw the worst of the floods, whilst earlier, in 1750, we learn that salmon was very cheap. It is from Neasham that the Tees takes a sweeping southerly loop which, when viewed on the map, reminds one of a Christmas stocking filled with the customary apple and orange.

A minor cul de sac road runs down to Sockburn Hall which is private and which has a legend, the Sockburn Worm, allegedly slain by Sir John Conyers. His falchion or broadsword is now in Durham cathedral library. What may be of greater interest to the literary minded is the fact that Wordsworth met his future wife, Mary Hutchinson, at nearby eighteenth century Sockburn Farm. Coleridge also visited the farm and set his sights on sister Sara, but to no avail for he was already married and so left Sockburn, only recording his love in his private diary. From Neasham the road meanders north to Dinsdale before turning south again to the river at our next port of call.

Middleton One Row

On a minor road from Dinsdale south of the A67, east from Darlington.
As the name implies this is literally a one-row village with houses on one side of the street and grassy slopes to the river on the other. Along the open side of the street people have been observed sitting in their cars munching their sandwiches and reading a paper or a novel, perhaps in the mistaken belief that they are at the seaside, such is the appeal of the place. Architecturally it has little to commend it and its elevated aspect above the river is certainly its greatest asset. Middleton is one of the places that should not be missed.

By taking the Aislaby road in the direction of Yarm, you will note a minor road left leading to an isolated church which serves the outlying farming community. At the time of writing a community task force was re-decorating the church. These people get everywhere - Killhope Wheel, village churches - they are certainly very thick on the ground.

A little way on along the same road is Low Middleton Hall which dates from the seventeen hundreds and which has a pigeon house of interesting proportions, an eight-sided structure with some 1500 nesting holes. Though the property is private it can be seen to advantage from the riverside path.

Before returning to Darlington another short diversion can be made to Middleton St George where Teesside Airport is located. Lacking the bustle of Heathrow or Gatwick one can, in comparative ease, indulge in flights of fancy whilst observing air travel at its leisurely best.

The Coast -
From Crimdon to Seaham

At Crimdon Beck you enter Durham from Cleveland and at the northern extremity of Hartlepool's North Sands is the holiday caraven park sited on the best cliffs along this stretch is the coastal landmark in these parts. There is public access to the beach.

The main road, the A1086, continues north to Blackhall Rocks where again there is beach access, then in Blackhall Colliery village one is reminded of New York since the streets are numbered rather than named. There could be an interesting study made of street names and one wonders whether a lack of imagination or some deliberate plan has resulted in Fourth and Fifth Street running off Middle Street. It is as though in some of these villages they have declared UDI and shown a respectful disregard for the world outside.

In the dip between Blackhall and Horden is the Castle Eden Dene Nature Reserve which is described in the Countryside Section and which is a blessed relief in a rather desolate moonscape.

At Horden you can turn seaward to observe a local 'pastime', more an occupation really. This is the business of winning coal from the sea after the manner of local fishermen using the haaf net in river estuaries. Before describing it further, here is a point on which to ponder. At least one north-east miner has used his redundancy money to purchase a trawler and he now harvests 'fruits-de-mer'. With coal mines running five, six and seven miles under the sea, this miner has transferred his energies to what lies in the sea rather than below it.

You should be suitably shod to observe the coal operation on the beach for it is muddy and mucky. The men wade into the water and, using nets, scoop up the coal which is constantly being washed ashore. They nevertheless have to read all the 'wave and weather signs' to determine whether it will be a good working day. It is then loaded on to old four-wheel-drive Army trucks which appear to break down quite frequently. They then cross the beach rather like someone following a secret trail through a swamp and climb, ever so slowly, the bank to the main road.

The quality of the coal is not A1 and it has a limited use in furnaces, but it also serves another purpose. It provides employment and income, however meagre, for people who are still able to work. And where does it come from? Is it the rubbish discharged from the nearby colliery or is there an underground seam being worked by King Neptune which British Coal hasn't yet discovered? With an estimated 500 million tons of coal under the North Sea it is likely that beach coaling will continue for quite some time.

Easington Colliery village was the scene of perhaps the worst mining disaster of modern times when in 1951 some eighty men were either killed or entombed. They are remembered in the local church of the Ascension and buried in a garden of memory in the local cemetery. The colliery is a huge complex and dominates the whole scene in these parts. To read of the life lived by the old miners in the days when real hardship was endured is a fascinating exercise and one which strikes the conscience. Easington itself is on higher ground, the church being a landmark for miles around, and though Norman in origin it was extensively restored in the nineteenth century. A number of prominent politicians have represented Easington in Parliament. The best known is probably 'Manny' Shinwell.

Continuing north on a stretch of the A19 trunk road there is a slip road into Seaham which is perhaps the nearest one will get to a seaside town on this Durham coast.

Seaham Harbour was the brainchild of the third Marquis of Londonderry whose equestrian statue stands in Durham market place. John Tweed's bronze statue of the same gentleman in the guise of Charles Van-Tempest-Stewart stands on the green in front of the former company offices - now the police station. Whilst his ambitious plans for the harbour came to fruition those for the town did not, and as a consequence one is left with the impression that things might have been different. Before trying to appreciate the complexities of the various harbours one should read a little of Seaham's history from say Thompson or Thorold. Today the fishing fleet is sadly depleted and a huge combine owns the harbour, a fact which has not been accepted too kindly by some of the locals who have seen the dues raised considerably. The Marquis also sunk a mine, the Vane-Tempest Colliery north of Seaham itself, and close by is the old church of Saxon origin, Saint Mary the Virgin. Keys to view the

SEAHAM HARBOUR

church are available from the farm and there will not be many Saxon churches overlooked by spoil heaps and a colliery!

In common with other locations along the coast Seaham has its quota of denes along which one can walk down to the beach. In this area there does happen to be cleaner sand which would have pleased Byron who apparently walked along the beach before tying the marital knot. He married a local lass, Anne Isabella Millbanke, in the drawing room of nearby Seaham Hall, but it was not to last. In fact, the wretched man satirised her most objectionably as Lady Millpond in Don Juan. The hall latterly became a hospital but today it serves as a hotel.

Mother Nature has been kind to the most northerly stretch of the county's coastline which is in sharp contrast to the beaches further south. It appears to have more affinity with near neighbour Northumberland, except that tourists are conspicuous by their absence. A picnic site with extensive views of the coast has been developed on the cliffs.

Within a short distance the county boundary is reached and you are in the district of Sunderland, actually at Ryhope, which has an attraction all of its own, a pumping engine. Like Papplewick, near Nottingham, Wigan and several other places, Ryhope has a restored engine which is open to the public, generally at weekends between Easter and December. If you drop in at any preservation society's showplace, be it locomotives or beam engines, you will invariably find posters for their fellow members.

Returning south on the A19 the best-known town lying between the trunk road and the coast is Peterlee which we will now consider.

Peterlee

Ten miles east of Durham City and ten miles north of Hartlepool skirted by the A19 and the A1086.

Peter Lee who gave his name to the town was a Durham man; a miner for most of his working life he was also much travelled in America and South Africa. In his time he had been chairman of the local co-op, the waterboard, and eventually the county council. He died in 1935 and is buried in Wheatley Hills cemetery. A facsimile of his signature will be found on the foundation stone of the first house to be built. Peterlee followed the normal pattern for New Towns and in 1947 John Silkin, the then Minister of Town and Country Planning, gave approval for the creation of a town of 30,000 inhabitants over the next twenty years. It would also develop opportunities for employment because the surrounding villages were so coal orientated that the inevitable dangers associated with a single industry were imminent.

As mentioned earlier, the shopping centre does appear to have some quite gusty corners but then so do many other places of similar design. The Information Centre has a dual role; as a tourist bureau and booking office and a place where all kinds of local queries can be handled. Parade names have a local connection, Yoden being the site of a nearby Saxon village and Chare being the Peterlee version of wynd or alley.

Church-goers are catered for by the three main denominations: the Anglicans at the brick-built Saint Cuthbert's church in the shape of an early basilica; the Catholic church has a prominent, slender copper spire; whilst the Methodist church carries the name of the outstanding Peter Lee, himself a Methodist local preacher.

If you plan to walk the whole Castle Dene Trail, then you could start from Peterlee.

Penshaw Monument

North of the junction of the A182 (Washington highway) and the A183 and close to Penshaw village.

Though now in Tyne and Wear, this is so prominent a landmark and so connected with much that is County Durham that it will not be out of place here. It was erected as a 'thank you' to the first Earl of Durham, John George Lambton, and as one can see it was after the design of the Grecian Temple of Theseus - actually twice its size. The now blackened sandstone is more Durham than Greek and when the foundation stone was laid in 1844 some 10,000 people came to watch the ceremony.

The practice of climbing to its summit for the extensive views was stopped after the inevitable tragedy. A youngster fell from its top and was killed. Will the National Trust who now own the monument pull it down or leave it as an inverted compliment to the builders? What with the Lambton Worm and the Penshaw Monument who needs space invaders, ET and the like?

Sedgefield

On the A177 ten miles north of Stockton-on-Tees.

The racing fraternity will know exactly where Sedgefield lies since it boasts a racecourse - the only one in Durham. The tourist too will have little difficulty in finding the place which is about equidistant between Durham and Stockton and on the cross-country route from Bishop Auckland to Hartlepool, the A689.

Sedgefield has been both village and town apparently at the whim of the local administration and made more confusing since 1974 when the offices of the Sedgefield District Council were established at, would you believe, Spennymoor. Perhaps Surtees in 1832 got it right when he described Sedgefield as 'a small, neat, market town with the appearance of a handsome village'.

In keeping with so many villages it is the church which is the focal point, it being sited in the most prominent place. Dedicated to St Edmund, it dates from the thirteenth century and has a splendid tower, a landmark which was added in the fifteenth century by a man of means who also gave Newcastle its cathedral tower. The real joy of the church is the Restoration woodwork in the form of panelling, traceried canopies, screens and later the eighteenth century organ case. Like so many churches in the county it can boast an example of Frosterley marble.

The Old Rectory has been acquired by the authorities for community activities and not surprisingly has been re-named Ceddesfield Hall, after the old name for Sedgefield.

Having for many years a population of some two thousand, Sedgefield has in recent times nearly trebled that with the influx of young executives and the like who are prepared to commute to the industrial black spots of Hartlepool, Stockton and Middlesbrough, rather than live there. In educational terms the daily influx of children from the outlying area has necessitated the building of larger schools. There is a quiet backwater of old people's residences and a couple of duck ponds which add a little colour to the rural image, though they are in fact hidden from general view.

In common with a small number of towns and villages - for instance, Ashbourne the ancient Shrove Tuesday football game has been played since the thirteenth century. Is it coincidence, one wonders, that the church was also built about this time?

The buildings of character date from the late seventeenth and early eighteenth centuries with the Queen Anne Manor House being perhaps the most prominent. Today it is the magistrates' court and sub-office of the district council. The Roman Catholic church could be overlooked, unless one was attending it, for it is wedged between houses and not easily identified. The inns are more noticeable, the Hardwick Arms being the former coaching inn in the era when it was necessary to travel by horse bus to the station, which was over a mile away. Dotted around Britain are railway stations which supposedly serve nearby towns and villages. They were usually located in these most inconvenient places because the squire, Duke or whoever considered them an abomination.

Since the building of the by-pass the village has acquired a reasonable calm, devoid of the heavy traffic which for years rumbled through its centre. In close proximity is Hardwick Hall, a popular spot with picnickers and the like since the development of a Country Park in the grounds. Originally the site of a fifteenth century manor house and later a Georgian building of no special merit, it is now a popular hotel much in demand for weddings and functions. The history of Hardwick from the time John Burden acquired it in 1748 is quite interesting. In keeping with the fashion of the day his landscaping included an artificial lake, a hermitage, a mock ruin, bath house and temple. Whilst all this was much admired by the Victorian tourist it was a sorry sight when it began to fall into disrepair. Reading the Hardwick Hall story one learns that it was once a hostel for Bevin Boys and later a maternity hospital, but there is no apparent connection!

There are two well-known hospitals on the northern side of Sedgefield which appear to suffer, at the time of writing, the effects of pollution from the nearby coking plant. With the wind in the wrong direction both the village of Fishburn and the hospitals will be obliged to endure some discomfort. A massive land reclamation scheme is being executed at Fishburn but the coking plant itself is apparently there to stay.

PENSHAW
MONUMENT

The Countryside in County Durham

A station announcement at York might run thus: 'All change for Durham', which is exactly what has been happening to that oft maligned county. Anyone looking for pastures new, for walking, bird watching and similar pleasures should try Durham.

Call first at the County Planning Department in County Hall, Durham City, and before collecting the numerous helpful leaflets take a look at the certificates on display. Awards from various bodies for excellent work in the fields of conservation and especially reclamation have been received. These include commendations from the EEC and a recent press item announced that Deerness Valley Walk along an old railway line had won a first prize as a conservation area.

There is an added attraction in these walks in that not only are they pleasant exercises in themselves, but they invariaby offer some attraction. At Shildon for instance, the Urban Trails are obviously closely linked to the railway story. At the Causey Arch Picnic Site is another historical location whilst those around High and Low Force offer river scenery at its best.

There is a very healthy agricultural picture in County Durham with almost half a million sheep grazing in beautiful countryside. If you come across what look like pit ponies put out to grass you will be delighted to learn that in mid 1985 the last of the working ponies in Durham was brought to the surface at Sacriston Colliery.

For the novice and the gregarious there are guided walks of about three miles in length and under three hours duration. What better in the last week of December than 'an antidote to Christmas over-indulgence'? The November to April list of walks is perhaps for the more hardy types especially with such titles as Winter Woodlands, Winter Wildlife and Winter Wander. The April to October leaflet also has some interesting walks on offer, some led by ecologists, local historians, archaeologists, archivists and naturalists. You pays your money and takes your pick. Another innovation in conjunction with coach operators might also interest you. These are the Ride and Ramble coach tours which are exactly what they say. They combine an eighty mile coach tour and a six mile ramble on one of the many attractive walks and if you are a car driver for most of the week then this could make a refreshing change. The 'Ride and Ramble Coach Tours' leaflet has all the details.

It was suggested that you approach Wolsingham via Hamsterley Forest where you can enjoy a four and a half mile drive. In the Visitor Centre is a static exhibition which explains forestry and which should interest young and old alike. The town dweller, and may be even the country one, will learn how to distinguish betwen a Sitka spruce, a Scots pine and a Douglas fir. Do have change handy - it's cheaper at the toll machine than paying in the office.

For the serious and well-equipped walker there are some remoter areas of the high fells, but a cautionary note is made for the inexperienced. A code of practice is set out very clearly in 'Safety on the Durham Fells', particularly with regard to clothing, preparation and procedure. There are two important danger signals: one concerns old lead mining shafts and buildings and the other refers to Army exercise grounds. Do not investigate the former and keep away from the latter where red flags fly and warning notices are displayed. Weather wise, the rule in these parts of the Pennines appears to be 'Be prepared for the Worst'.

Put kindly, quite a number of us haven't much of a clue when it comes to countryside matters and an invaluable leaflet for such people is 'Understanding the Durham countryside'. Not only does it cover such aspects as farming, village greens, moors, boundaries, holes in the ground and power, but it contrasts the old with the new.

Two extremely good information packs are Country Walks and Railway Walks, both on waterproof route cards and a handy pocket size. On the Waskerley Way, an 1834 railway line, is Nanny Mayor's incline. How fitting that a stretch of line should be named after so popular a lady - she kept an ale house by the side of the line! On Lanchester Valley Walk at Malton, German engineers built a benzine works by the colliery. Ironically, bombers piloted by their fellow countrymen destroyed it in World War II.

On one of the country walks you will pass a shooting lodge where the Queen Mother spent part of her honeymoon. This is the Earl of Strathmore's shooting house, Holwick Lodge, in the Bowlees and Low Force area. Also from here you have one of those difficult decisions to make if you are so inclined; it is 144 miles from Edale and 126 miles from Kirk Yetholm if you would like to experience the Pennine Way.

These two packs are real value for money and together with the Walkabout Leaflets are a credit to the Countryside Team which produces them. Credit too to the Peterlee Development Corporation for their leaflet on the Castle Eden Dene local nature reserve, but more especially to the combined efforts of the four groups concerned. These are Easington District Council, Durham County Council, Peterlee Town Council and the Development Corporation who have agreed, with the assistance of a scientific advisory committee, to ensure that the flora and fauna of the Dene should be protected and preserved. There are 26 features listed on the leaflet and with access so close to Peterlee town centre it provides a haven of relaxation literally on the doorstep. Just under four miles long it is the largest of the county's coastal ravines and a favourite with country lovers.

The attention to detail is perhaps best seen in the four seasonal leaflets produced for the Collier Wood Nature Trail, two miles south of Tow Law. In spring you are invited to study the looper caterpillar arching its way along branches. In summer the footprints of badger, vole and hedgehog will help you identify these animals whilst the changing bird population is described in the autumn leaflet. The winter story reminds us that birds like the tree creeper are easy to spot when the leaves have been shed. The Conservation Trust is to be congratulated for their efforts in making these informative leaflets available to the public.

The saga of Country Parks and picnic areas in County Durham is a continuing one for the leaflets are usually dotted with such statements as 'due to open in March 19--'. In fact, the last published information sheet could now be out of date and one should enquire if any new additions have been made. At the time of writing there were listed some 29 with another four short-stay sites for travellers on major routes. The main ones include such delightful names as Hanging Shaw, Toytop, Windy Nook and Pow Hill. Whereas Durham was once remembered as a county one passed through en route to somewhere more interesting, today the image has changed. It is an area one should be thinking of going to rather than through.

CAUSEY ARCH

Mike Brown.

INDEX